Good Citizenship Counts

FEATURING INDIVIDUAL STORYBOOKS ON:
- *Being a good citizen*
- *Obeying rules and laws*
- *Being considerate of others*
- *Respecting the property of others*
- *Being honest*
- *Respecting all people*
- *Being responsible*
- *Sharing and taking turns*
- *Conserving our resources*
- *Taking care of your body*

BY LINDA D. HAGLER

©2003 YouthLight, Inc.

*Dedicated
to all the
parents and teachers
who work to build
good citizenship
in children.*

— LINDA D. HAGLER

Table of Contents

How to use this guide 4

Why Focus on Citizenship 5

Story Lesson Guides:

1. *What's a Good Citizen Anyway?*
   Being a good citizen 7

2. *Why Obey Rules?*
   Obeying rules and laws 12

3. *The Magic of Good Manners*
   Being considerate of others 17

4. *Grandpa's Knife*
   Respecting the propery of others 22

5. *The Best Story Ever*
   Being Honest 29

6. *Everyone Is Special*
   Respecting all people 36

7. *D.C.'s Adventure*
   Being Responsible 41

8. *That's Mine! Keep Your Hands Off*
   Sharing and taking turns 47

9. *Can I Help Save the World?*
   Conserving our resources 53

10. *No Bath Tonight*
    Taking care of your body 58

Certificate of Completion 68

©2003 YouthLight, Inc.

INTRODUCTION:

Good Citizenship Counts

These books were written to help students become more aware of the rights and responsibilities they have as citizens of families, schools, communities, states, countries, and the world. It is my belief that we must teach our children that all people are equal and worthy of their respect. We must teach them that by working together and practicing good citizenship, our world can be a happier, healthier and safer place to live.

How To Use The Program

This program is designed to be used by parents or in a classroom setting. It contains ten individual stories that deal with ten different aspects of citizenship. The stories can easily be read by upper elementary school students or shared orally in the lower elementary grades. Each story is followed by thought provoking questions that can be used by the educators or the parents. Varying activities such as games, story and poem writing, discussions, or music are included for each story in the program.

©2003 YouthLight, Inc.

Why Focus On Citizenship

According to Webster's Dictionary, a citizen is a native, inhabitant, or denizen of a town or city. He or she is a member of a state or nation and owes allegiance to it and is entitled to full civil rights either by birth or by naturalization. A person residing away from the country of which he is or once was a citizen is often referred to as a national by fellow countrymen.

Closely related to citizenship are the concepts of patriotism and nationalism. Patriotism is the love and loyal support of one's country. Nationalism is devotion or complete loyalty to one's nation.

Patriotism includes an emotional attachment for the people of a country. It encourages admiration for customs and traditions of one's country, pride in its history, and devotion to its welfare. All these things promote a feeling of membership in a nation. Our schools and families help to develop a love for country through the study of history as children are taught an appreciation for common hopes, memories, and traditions of their country. Patriotism carries with it a responsibility for public service from all citizens. Patriotic citizens have a duty to be informed on public issues, take part in civic affairs, and to contribute to the welfare of their country. World travel, as it has developed through the years has added a new dimension to patriotism. Many people now reside in countries distant from the countries of their birth and earn their livings in these foreign countries. Are they to love the land of their ancestors, the land of their birth, or the country in which they now live? This can raise the questions of to which country they owe their allegiance or is it possible to be patriotic to both a new country and the land of their birth.

Nationalism also promotes the sense of belonging together as a nation. It promotes loyalty to the nation and pride in its history. Nationalism grew as a nation state — a group of people who shared a common history or language, resided in a common area of land, and had an independent government. Travel and communication increased and people became more aware of countries outside their own communities. There became stronger allegiances to kings or rulers and less loyalty to religious and local leaders. This was evidenced in the 1800s when Americans became convinced that their nation should claim all of the North American Continent for its own territory. In the 1930s Adolph Hitler and Benito Mussolini practiced extreme nationalism as they demanded unfaltering loyalty from the people of their countries. They promoted integral nationalism — the belief that a certain nationality was superior to all others. This resulted

©2003 YouthLight, Inc.

in the slaughter of millions of Jews and other people whom they considered to be inferior.

Nationalism's effects can be both good and bad. It gives people a sense of belonging. It instills them with pride and makes them willing to make sacrifices for their country. However, it also produces rivalry and tension between and within nations. Desires for national glory and military conquest may lead to war. Extreme nationalism may result in racial hatred and persecution or minority groups.

Even though we use all of these terms to identify with one's nation, we, as differing nationalities, make up the world's citizenship. On September 11, 2001, the United States fell victim to the horror of terrorist attacks. It has become increasingly evident that we as an entire world — a world in which man has the ability to eat breakfast on one continent and dinner on another, the ability to destroy entire cities with a missile from halfway around the world, and the capabilities to spread germ warfare to thousands of people on another continent — must learn how to live together in harmony. To do so, we must teach our children that they are citizens not just of their countries but of the world. We must teach them that they are worthy of respect regardless of their nationality, their race, or religion. In return they must learn that all other people of the world are worthy of that same respect. This respect for others begins in the home as we teach our very young children to recognize and appreciate the uniqueness of each family member and help them to accept individual strengths and weaknesses. We must teach them to cooperate in a harmonious manner while still allowing them the freedom to question authority with respect and make their own individual decisions. This teaching must then extend into our classrooms, our neighborhoods, our cities, states, countries, and ultimately our world. Good citizenship does count.

STORY 1

What's A Good Citizen Anyway?

©2003 YouthLight, Inc.

SUMMARY:

Antoine and his mother are in the post office when Antoine notices the pictures of men hanging on the wall. He asks his mother who they are and she tells him that they are men wanted by the FBI. His mother stresses that these men are not good citizens. This leads to a discussion defining citizenship. His mother points out that we are citizens of families, classrooms, communities, states, nations, and the world. She stresses the importance of abiding by the established rules and laws so that our society will be peaceful.

ACTIVITIES:

1. **Share the book:**
   What's a Good Citizen Anyway?
   Lead a discussion of the meaning of the word citizen.
   According to Webster's Dictionary, a citizen is:
   (a) formerly, a native or inhabitant, especially a freeman or burgess.
   (b) loosely, a native, inhabitant, or denizen of any place.
   (c) a member of a state or nation especially one with a republican form of government, who owes allegiance to it by birth or naturalization and is entitled to full civil rights.

2. **Prepare and display this poster:**
   Citizenship is:
   - Having good manners
   - Respecting authority
   - Using kind words
   - Accepting responsibility for your actions
   - Doing what you can to make your home, school, and neighborhood a better place.

3. **Good Citizen Quilt:**
   Give each child an 8" by 8" square of paper. Have him/her draw a self-portrait on the paper. On the bottom of the paper, have him/her write a sentence telling what he does that shows he/she is a good citizen. Put the pictures together to make a Good Citizen quilt to display in your classroom or an adjacent hallway.

STORY 1

What's A Good Citizen Anyway?

©2003 YouthLight, Inc.

4. Government Official:
Invite a local government official, such as the mayor, to speak to the class about the importance of good citizenship. Before the guest's visit, explain to him/her that your class has been studying good citizenship skills and that you would like for him to address these skills during the visit. Before the visit, allow each student to make up three questions he/she would like to ask the guest. Younger students may need to rehearse their questions. After the guest leaves, make a list of ways the visitor shows he/she is a good citizen. Guide the students in writing thank-you cards for the visitor.

5. Good Citizenship Banner:
During class meeting time, brainstorm with the students citizenship goals they could adopt for one week. These might be: walking quietly in the hall, using good table manners, helping to clean the room, etc.. Choose one goal for the week. Give each child a piece of white drawing paper. Instruct him/her to draw their picture on the paper. Secure the completed pictures to a long piece of bulletin board paper, leaving an empty spot in the middle of the bulletin board paper. Laminate the paper with the pictures on it. In the blank center part of the laminated paper, write the citizenship goal for the week. As you observe the students behaving as good citizens, add their names under their pictures. At the end of the week, erase the names and the goal for the week. Begin with a new goal the next week.

6. Citizenship books:
(a) Inform parents of citizenship study.
(b) Ask parents to send old magazines and newspapers to class
(c) Allow students to scan the newspapers and magazines to find and cut out articles or pictures showing people who are demonstrating good citizenship, such as workers for Habitat for Humanity, Community Litter Pick-ups, Elections, or Charity Walks.
(d) Allow the students to make booklets of their selected pictures. Under each picture have them write a sentence telling why the pictured person is a good citizen.

7. Citizenship Chain:
(a) Talk about what makes a person a good citizen.
(b) Give each child a 12" by 1 1/2" strip of paper.
(c) Have each child write a sentence on the strip telling something that makes a good citizen.
(d) Glue the first strip into a circle.
(e) Add the other strips, making a sentence chain.

ACTIVITY SHEET 1.1

What's A Good Citizen Anyway?

©2003 YouthLight, Inc.

Being a Good Citizen

Citizen Choices:

Read each sentence. Circle Yes if you think a good citizen would act this way. Circle No if you do not think a good citizen would act this way. Then, on the back of your paper, rewrite each NO statement so that it becomes a YES statement.

1. Bet asked Lib if she could jump rope with her at playtime. Lib said, "No, you miss too much." Is Lib being a good citizen? .... Yes   No

2. Vicky sees that Billy has no more glue. She says, "Here, Billy, you may use my glue." Is Vicky being a good citizen? .... Yes   No

3. Bobby always has to be first in line. Is he being a good citizen? .... Yes   No

4. Sue's school is voting on new school uniforms. Sue says she does not have time to vote. When the uniforms are chosen, Sue does not like them. She complains. Is she being a good citizen? .... Yes   No

5. Trace borrowed Bailey's airplane and lost it. He apologized and offered to pay for it. Was he being a good citizen? .... Yes   No

6. Mrs. Blake asked Don to take a message to the office for her. Don runs in the hall even though he knows it is against school rules. Is he being a good citizen? .... Yes   No

ACTIVITY SHEET 1.2

What's A Good Citizen Anyway?

©2003 YouthLight, Inc.

Being a Good Citizen

Read the following story to the class.
Ask the students the questions below for discussion.

Mrs. Black, a third grade teacher, asks Jamie and Clay to take some papers to Mr. Gray in another building of the school. On the way to Mr. Gray's class, Jamie runs in the hall. Clay follows the school rule and walks quietly. Then, Jamie goes into the boys' restroom to wash his hands. He leaves the water running. Clay goes in to turn off the water but then reminds Jamie that they are not supposed to go anywhere but to Mr. Gray's class. All the way back from Mr. Gray's class, Jamie runs in the hall. Clay reminds Jamie of the rules, but Jamie will not listen.

When the boys get back to Mrs. Black's class, she asks, "Did you both remember our good citizenship rules on the way to Mr. Gray's class? Jamie and Clay both answer, "Yes."

1. Do you think Jamie was acting like a good citizen in the hall? Why or why not?

2. Do you think Clay was acting like a good citizen in the hall? Why or why not?

3. How did Clay try to help Jamie while they were in the hall?

4. What do you think might have happened if Clay had not been there to turn off the water?

5. Do you think you would act like Jamie or Clay if your teacher sent you to take something to another classroom?

6. What should Jamie have done differently to show good citizenship?

7. Do you think Clay should have told the teacher what Jamie did on the way? Why or why not?

ACTIVITY SHEET 1.3

What's A Good Citizen Anyway?

©2003 YouthLight, Inc.

Being a Good Citizen

Please tell why you will choose to be a good citizen:

I will choose to be a good citizen because _____

_____

_____

_____

_____

_____

Write an acrostic for the word citizens:

C _____

I _____

T _____

I _____

Z _____

E _____

N _____

S _____

STORY 2

Why Obey Rules?

©2003 YouthLight, Inc.

SUMMARY:

In this story Ashley finishes her homework but fails to put it away as she has previously been directed to do. Her younger brother proceeds to find her homework and draws on it. Ashley discovers this just at the time for her favorite TV show, Captain Zelda. Her father informs her that she will have to redo her homework instead of watching TV. Ashley becomes very upset when she is told that she must abide by the family rules and insists that the world would be a better place with no rules. That night she dreams that there are no rules in her family, her town, or her school. By her dream she discovers that a world with no rules is definitely not the place to live.

ACTIVITIES:

1. **Define rule and law.**
   Ask the students if they know the difference between a rule and a law. Allow time to share their knowledge. Ask why they think there are rules and laws? Ask the students to write a short story about either The School With No Rules or The Town With No Laws. Allow time for the students to share their completed stories.

2. **Share the book, *Why Obey Rules?* with the students.**
   Discuss the rules that Ashley was not observing at the beginning of the story and the problems it caused. Then, discuss what happened in Ashley's dream. Why did she decide that rules were not so bad?

3. **Classroom Rules:**
   Have the students help make rules for the classroom and decide on consequences for breaking the rules. Make parents aware of the rules by having the students write them and put them in their agendas. *(Activity sheet 2.1)*

4. **Research:**
   Give older students an assignment to research the making of a law in their state or the nation.

5. **Newspaper Collages:**
   Allow students to search newspapers for examples of people who have broken the law. Have them cut out the articles and paste them onto a large classroom collage. Talk about the choices that the offenders in the articles made and the consequences of their choices. Have the students write a letter to an offender telling him/her about his/her bad choices. *(Activity sheet 2.2)*

6. **Field trip:**
Plan a field trip to a local courtroom to allow students to see the legal process at work.

7. **Field trip:**
For older students, plan a field trip to the adult jail or juvenile prison.

8. **Good choices and bad choices:**
Write the words, Think Before You Act, on the chalkboard. Allow the students to discuss its meaning. Discuss how people sometimes make bad choices because they have not thought about the consequences of bad behavior. Allow them to practice this concept by asking themselves questions such as these— ***"Is it kind? Is it safe? Is it healthy? What will be the consequences if I do this?"*** A chart could be made of these questions.

9. **Enjoy music:**
Sing to the tune of *"The Wheels on the Bus"* these songs:

The rules of the school,
Are to keep us safe,
Keep us safe,
Keep us safe,
The rules of the school,
They keep us safe,
Everyday at school.

The laws of the state,
Do protect all people,
Protect all people,
Protect all people,
The laws of the state,
Do protect all people,
And give them a safer life.

10. **Self- discipline:**
Lead younger students in a game of Simon Says. Tell the class to obey only the instructions that have the words "Simon Says" before them. Give instructions both with and without "Simon Says. These can be "raise a finger in the air, hop on one foot, Simon Says 'sit down.' After the game is over, discuss how they practiced self-discipline. Point out that keeping rules and laws is self- discipline.

ACTIVITY SHEET 2.1

Why Obey Rules?

©2003 YouthLight, Inc.

Our Classroom Rules

1. _____
2. _____
3. _____
4. _____
5. _____
6. _____

Consequences And Rewards

1. _____
2. _____
3. _____
4. _____
5. _____

ACTIVITY SHEET 2.2

Why Obey Rules?

©2003 YouthLight, Inc.

ACTIVITY SHEET 2.3

Why Obey Rules?

©2003 YouthLight, Inc.

Read the following stories. Answer YES if you think this is a person who is obeying rules or laws. If the person is not, circle NO. Then on the lines under the question please give him some advice to help him.

1. Mrs. Jones left the classroom for a moment. John got out of his seat and went over to Mark's desk to ask him a question.   YES   NO

   _____

2. Miss Curt is late for a visit with her doctor. The road sign says "speed limit 35". Miss Curt is driving 50 miles per hour because she is late.   YES   NO

   _____

3. Mitch found a five dollar bill on the floor of the classroom. He picked it up and gave it to the teacher.   YES   NO

   _____

4. Kisha went to the movies. When the movie she was seeing ended, she slipped into another movie at the theater and sat down.   YES   NO

   _____

5. Tonya wants to go home with Sidney. Mom said, "no." Tonya wrote her own note to Mr. Jones. It said, "Tonya may go to Sidney's house today."   YES   NO

   _____

STORY 3

The Magic of Good Manners

©2003 YouthLight, Inc.

SUMMARY:

Michelle, Mark, and Dan live with their very tired grandmother. The children have terrible table manners. After one evening meal Grandmother is expecting a guest. She looks at the mess on the floor and on the table. In her exasperation, she exclaims, "I wish I had a magic wand to clean up this mess." To her surprise, a magic wand appears and it's in the hand of a very old fairy. The fairy proceeds to grant Grandma a left over birthday wish. Grandma, of course, wishes for good table manners for her grandchildren. The little fairy takes the wish a bit further as she grants good manners to be used in other situations as well.

ACTIVITIES:

1. **Share the story:**
   Ask the students the meaning of the word manners. You might also introduce the word etiquette as its synonym. Ask them to tell good manners they use. List the examples on a chart. Invite the students to listen as you share the story The Magic of Good Manners. After the story is complete, discuss the attitudes of the characters at the beginning of the story and at the end. Lead them to conclude why and how the attitudes changed.

2. **Aladdin Bulletin Board:**
   Prepare an Aladdin, his lamp, and several puffs of smoke. Allow the students to think of good manners words such as "thank you, excuse me, pardon me, etc.." to write on the clouds. Put these above Aladdin's lamp on the bulletin board. Use the title, The Magic of Good Manners.

3. **Good Manners Sentences:**
   Instruct each child to complete this sentence on a sentence strip:
   Good manners help _____.
   Post these on a chart or the bulletin board.

4. **Place Mats:**
   Give each child a 12" x 18" piece of white construction paper. Have them decorate it as a place mat. Give them inexpensive paper plates, plastic utensils, paper cups, and napkins. Help them correctly place these on their placemats. Role play the correct way to use each of these. When finished with the role play, allow them to glue the paper pates, utensils, cup, and napkins to their placements.

17

STORY 3

The Magic of Good Manners

©2003 YouthLight, Inc.

5. **Obeying Good Manners Rules:**
   Make copies of the rules of good manners *(Activity sheet 3.1)* Cut them apart. Then place them in a container and allow each student to draw one out. Instruct him to draw a picture showing someone obeying the rule he drew from the container. When the students are finished, use the pictures to make a class "Good Manners" book. Allow students to share the completed book with other classes or younger students. Then put it on display in the media center.

6. **Passing the Buck:**
   Play this game with the students. Have everyone stand in a circle. The buck is a beanbag, a glove, or a small rubber ball. Toss the buck to a player in the circle. The person who catches the buck must give one rule of good manners. He or she then passes the buck to another student who must tell another good manners rule. Play continues in this manner.

7. **Poetry Writing:**
   Divide the students into groups of two. Allow half of the groups to write poems about a child who uses poor manners called Sloppy Sally. Instruct the other half of the groups to write poems about a child who uses good manners called Delightful Dora. Allow them to share their poetry when finished.

8. **Because:**
   (Activity Sheet 3.2 — Copy and cut the sentences apart.)
   (A) Have the students sit on the floor in a circle with their legs crossed.
   (B) Give a sentence to every third person. Instruct him not to show his sentence.
   (C) As the game begins, the person with the first sentence reads it. *(Ex. Bobby spoke with his mouth full.)* The person sitting by him must tell the reason why. *(Ex. He had exciting things to say.)* The third person in the circle must give the consequence. *(Ex. Bobby's neighbor was showered with food.)* The game continues in this manner until all have turns.

18

The Magic of Good Manners

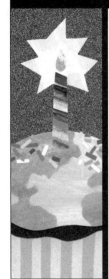

Rules for Good Manners

- Use spoons, forks, and knives to eat.
- Put your napkin on you lap — use it to wipe your mouth.
- Chew with your mouth closed.
- Sit upright in your chair.
- Keep elbows off the table.
- Answer "yes, please" for food you care for.
- Answer "no, thank you" for food you do not care for.
- Say "may I have some more please" to ask for more if all have been served.
- Say "may I be excused" before leaving the table.
- Do not interrupt when adults are talking.
- Do not walk between two people who are talking.
- Use the words "yes, ma'am or yes sir" when answering a woman or man.
- Say "thank you" when help is given.
- Wait your turn.
- Use the words "I'm sorry," when you are wrong or hurt someone.
- Be willing to share.

The Magic of Good Manners

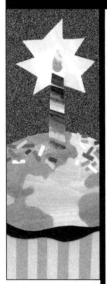

Good Manners Sentences

Juan ran in the hall at school.

Mrs. Evans and Mr. Black were talking. John walked between them.

Madison bumped Emily with her chair.

Bianca asks Brandy if she wants some green beans. Brandy does not like green beans and tells Bianca, "No, thank you.".

Mr. Jones asks, "Brett, do you have your homework?"

Britney burped aloud at lunch.

Janet ate her beans with her fingers.

Bobby spoke with food in his mouth.

Latasha bumped into Bill.

Ms. Green and Ms. Doe were talking and did not see Andy fall and hurt his knee. Jeff runs to the adults and says, "Please excuse me."

Mary Kate dropped all the markers. Tim is sitting by her.

Leon sits on the corner of his chair in the lunchroom.

Anthony yelled, "Clayvon, you are such a baby!"

Ann broke into the line at the water fountain.

Jackson is finished with his dinner and wants to go play.

Mr. Brown asked Craig if he would like some cherry ice cream. Craig loves cherry ice cream.

ACTIVITY SHEET 3.3

The Magic of Good Manners

©2003 YouthLight, Inc.

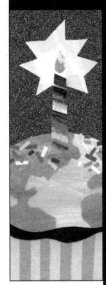

Complete each sentence.

1. This is Carly's first day at your school. At playtime, you see that she is standing by herself so _____.

2. The lunchroom is very noisy today. To show your best manners, you should _____ _____.

3. At the water fountain, you accidentally step on Chase's foot. You _____ _____.

4. The class is working on an art project. Ann bumps into you and causes you to drop the markers. She says, I'm sorry. You say, _____ _____.

5. Mike and you are very good friends. Mike has a new red bike. You would really like to ride it. When you go to Mike's house, the bike is in the driveway so _____ _____.

6. Mara brought cupcakes to school today. When she gives you one, _____ _____.

7. When you are eating lunch, you get spaghetti on your chin, you _____ _____.

8. Chris broke her pencil. You have two. You say _____ _____.

STORY 4

Grandpa's Knife

©2003 YouthLight, Inc.

SUMMARY:

Jamie and his friend Hosea have a favorite play area at a creek near their homes. One day as they are preparing to go play, Hosea notices a big knife lying on a chair in Jamie's house and insists that they take it to cut limbs to build a fort. The knife was a gift to Jamie's father from his grandfather. Jamie knows he should not take the knife but gives in to peer pressure. All morning the boys use the knife to build a fort. When the boys go home for lunch, the knife is left behind on a tree stump. When the boys return, the knife is gone. In the process of finding the knife, Jamie learns a lesson about respecting the property of others.

ACTIVITIES:

Respecting the property of others

1. **Share the book:**
   Discuss why Jamie was not anxious to get home for dinner. Allow the students to discuss their feelings about the actions of Jamie and Hosea as they took the knife out to cut branches discussing both the safety factor and the fact that Jamie did not respect his father's property. Ask the students to tell the meaning of the word **respect.** After they have discussed it, write the following meaning on a piece of chart paper. Respect is treating others as you would like to be treated. Respect is being considerate of the feelings of others. Respect is recognizing the value of property, people, our environment, and yourself. Put this up in the room so the students can see it. Write the words **integrity** and **honesty** on the chart also. Ask if anyone knows the meaning of these two words. Write this meaning for integrity on the chart. Integrity means being strong enough to do what you know is right. Integrity means knowing the difference between wrong and right and choosing to do the right thing, even when it is difficult. Ask the students if Jamie showed integrity in the story. Allow them to discuss their answers. Write this meaning for honesty on the chart. Honesty means you tell the truth. Honesty means you do not cheat, steal, or lie. Ask the class if Jamie showed honesty in the story. Discuss the importance of each of the words in personal relationships.

2. **Historical People of Respect:**
   Have the students think of historical people who are known for their respect for the property, integrity, or honesty. If they can think of no one, point these out:

   A. <u>George Washington,</u> as the story goes, cut down his father's cherry tree with a hatchet His father was very angry about it. When he asked George about it, even though he knew he would be in trouble, he told the truth.

B. <u>Abe Lincoln,</u> as a child went to the store for his mother. When he was almost home, he found that the store clerk had given him too much change. He could have kept the money for himself, but he walked all the way back to the store to return the change. He did not keep something that was not his. From this time on, he was known as Honest Abe.

C. <u>Martin Luther King</u> saw that black people were not being treated fairly in the United States. He wanted black children to have the chance to go to good schools. He wanted black men and women to have good jobs. He wanted black families to have good houses. He knew his work would be difficult but he knew what he had to do. He was a man of integrity.

3. Respect For Property:
Ask the students how they can show respect for the property of others?
Listen to their suggestions and lead them to these conclusions:
   A. Ask before you borrow something.
   B. Some times the owner may not be willing to let you borrow something because it is special.
   C. Return a borrowed item to its owner in good condition and in a fair amount of time.
   D. If you should happen to break or lose a borrowed item, replace it.

Discuss the importance of each of the conclusions.

4. Storywriting:
Assign the story title, Hannah's Beautiful Book. Prompt them by saying for Hannah's birthday she was given a beautiful, new book by her aunt. Hannah was so proud of her book that she put it in her bookbag and took it to school. Have the students write a story about what happened to the book at school. Allow time for them to share their stories. *(Activity sheet 4.2)*

5. Song:
If We Borrow Something — sung to the tune of *London Bridge*

If we borrow something,
We must give it back,
Give it back,
Give it back.
If we borrow something,
We must give it back,
To the one who owns it.

If we lose or break something,
We have borrowed,
We have borrowed,
We have borrowed,
If we lose or break something
We have borrowed,
Then we must replace it.

STORY 4

Grandpa's Knife

©2003 YouthLight, Inc.

6. **Golden Rule:**
   Ask the students if anyone has ever heard of the Golden Rule. If not, tell them that the Golden Rule is this: "Do unto others as you would have them do unto you." Discuss the meaning of this. Remind the students that it was written long ago to remind people to show respect. Ask if Jamie and Hosea followed this rule in the story. What should they have done? Give each child a 12" by 18" piece of paper. Have them write the Golden Rule in the center. Have them draw and color frames along the edges of their papers. Allow them to take these home to hang.

7. **Acrostic:**
   Ask the students to write acrostics using the words respect, property, integrity or honesty. *(Activity sheet 4.1)*

8. **Respect Others' Property Song:**
   Put the words to this song on a poster.
   Sing it to the tune of *"Row, Row, Row Your Boat"*:

   Respect, respect, respect the things
   That belong to other folks,
   Please don't touch, oh, please don't touch,
   Unless you're told to do so.

9. **Divide the class into partners.**
   Ask them to write poems about one of these topics:
   HONESTY, INTEGRITY, RESPECT. Allow time for sharing.

10. **Have the students write letters:**
    Write to Jamie telling him what they think he should have done in the story. *(Activity sheet 4.4)*

11. **Have the students pretend that they are Jamie.**
    Have them write a thank you note to Dad for being understanding instead of angry.

12. **Have the students role play...**
    Examples of repecting the property of others, integrity, and honesty.
    (Examples for the role play are given on Activity sheet 4.3)

ACTIVITY SHEET 4.1

Grandpa's Knife

©2003 YouthLight, Inc.

Make an acrostic for one of these words: <u>Respect</u> for property, <u>Integrity</u>, or <u>Honesty</u>.

ACTIVITY SHEET 4.2

Grandpa's Knife

©2003 YouthLight, Inc.

Write a story. Pretend that Hannah brought her beautiful book to school. Tell what happened as she shared her book.

Hannah's Beautiful Book

_____
_____
_____
_____
_____
_____
_____
_____
_____
_____
_____

Draw a picture of Hannah's book:

ACTIVITY SHEET 4.3

Grandpa's Knife

©2003 YouthLight, Inc.

Divide into groups and role play these situations:

Situation 1:
Sandy and John are twins. They sit beside each other in class. They both like to buy a cookie at lunch. Their parents only allow them to buy a cookie once a week. One morning when John was at the water fountain, he found 35 cents. That was just enough for a cookie at lunch. Sandy knew John had already bought his cookie for the week. Finish the story by acting it out.

Situation 2:
Beth and her friends Lindsay and Cleo always stop at the neighborhood store. One afternoon while at the store, Beth saw Lindsay put some candy in her pocket without paying for it. Lindsay whispered to Cleo, "Take some candy. We won't get caught."

Cleo grabbed some candy and put it in her pocket, but Beth said, "We have to pay for the candy. Stealing is wrong. If you don't pay for it or put it back, I am going to tell the store owner what you did." Finish the story by acting it out.

Situation 3:
Dan went to the store for his mother. His mom had given him $5.00. She said, "Dan, I don't have time to go to the store. If you will go and buy some milk and bread for me, you may have the rest of the money."

At the store Dan got the bread and milk. When the cashier rung up the total, it was $2.98. That meant Dan would be getting back $2.02. However, when she gave Dan the money, she gave him $4.02. Finish the story by acting it out.

Situation 4:
Don has $10.00 that he has been saving to buy a new video. He borrowed a CD from Clay and left it in the sun. The CD will no longer play. The CD cost $7.99. Finish the story by acting it out.

Situation 5:
Tomika sits next to Arthur in class. Arthur has a lot of trouble with spelling. On Friday, when Mrs. Black started the spelling test, Tomika saw that Authur had his list of spelling words under his test paper and was looking at the words. Finish the story by acting it out.

ACTIVITY SHEET 4.4

Grandpa's Knife

©2003 YouthLight, Inc.

Write a letter to Jamie telling him how you feel about his actions in this story.

STORY 5

The Best Story Ever

©2003 YouthLight, Inc.

SUMMARY:

Margo's teacher gives the class a writing assignment. Margo has difficulty deciding upon a topic for her writing. She thinks and thinks. Then she reads the story of her friend Shan. Margo likes Shan's story so much that she develops her own story using the very same idea that Shan used. She even uses the same illustrations. This results in Mrs. Baker, the teacher, asking Margo to stay inside at playtime. Mrs. Baker confronts Margo with her suspicions that her work was not original. Margo learns a valuable lesson about being honest.

ACTIVITIES:

Being Honest

1. **Talk it over:**
   Ask the students what it means to be honest. List any examples they give you on chart paper. After they have shared their ideas, write the following sentences on the chart: Someone who tells the truth is honest. Someone who is honest does not cheat, steal or lie. Then share the book, *The Best Story Ever*. Discuss with the students the actions of Margo. Point out that the experience Margo had of not being able to think does happen to most people at some time. Ask them for suggestions of what Margo could have done. Ask them if Margo cheated. (With young children cheating may need to be explained.) Ask them if Margo lied. Ask them if Margo stole. (Here, too, you may need to point out that she did steal Shan's thoughts for her own story and illustrations.)

2. **Analyze the characters:**
   Do a character analysis of Margo, Shan, and Mrs. Baker. Have each student write descriptive words for each of them. When each student is finished, do a group chart of the descriptive words they used and discuss them. Be sure to include Margo's feelings about herself that were evident when she did not want Shan to see her work and when she did not want her dad to know. *(Activity sheet 5.1)*

3. **Character Chart:**
   Put the name of a celebrity, politician, a TV character, sports figure or team at the top of a character chart. Students should be asked to discuss if the celebrity is honest or not honest. Have a class discussion of activities, actions, or life decisions the celebrities either have or have not made that would allow them to be honored or discredited as someone who lives honestly. When singers, TV stars, sports

STORY 5

The Best Story Ever

©2003 YouthLight, Inc.

figures, or politicians are used, there should be lively discussions because of the knowledge the students possess about them. Have them discuss the consequences of the actions of the celebrities. Write these on the poster. Point out that actions have consequences. *(Activity Sheet 5.1)*

4. Character Chart for Historical figures:
For a social studies activity, keep a chart of historical leaders. *(Activity Sheet 5.1 can be used for this)* Record the reason and the consequences. Have the students summarize each character by writing a sentence showing their honesty or dishonesty.

5. Character Analysis of Fairy Tale Characters:
For younger students, use classic fairy tale characters from books such as *The Three Little Pigs, Hansel and Gretel, Jack and the Beanstalk, Little Red Riding Hood,* or *The Gingerbread Man.* Read a story to the students. Then discuss each of the characters allowing the students to conclude which were honest and which were dishonest. Again, point out the consequences of the choices made by the characters.

6. Margo's Story:
Have the students write Margo's story about the little girl who learned a lesson about cheating.

7. Honesty Stories:
Have the students write about a time they were proud because they behaved honestly. *(Activity sheet 5.2)*

8. Honest Looks Like List:
Have the students make a list of what honesty looks like in the classroom. Older students should do this first alone and then combine the list as a whole group activity. Younger students should do this as a group activity. Be sure to take this opportunity to discuss classroom rules, school rules, and laws of the country.

9. "If you're Honest and You Know It":
Sing this song to the tune of *"If You're Happy and You Know It."*
If you're honest and you know it, Clap your hands,
If you're honest and you know it, Clap your hands.
If you're honest and you know it,
Then your actions will surely show it,
If you're honest and you know it, clap your hands.

10. Honesty Pledge Banners:
Give each child a 12" by 18" piece of construction paper. Cut an 18" piece of yarn for each banner. Tie the ends of the yarn together. Have the children fold one 12" side of the paper under one inch. Place the yarn in the folded end and glue the fold in place. Cut the other 12" end of the paper in banner style. On the paper have each student write Honesty Pledge at the top. Then have each student write 3 things he/she can do to show he/she is honest. Allow them to decorate the banners with crayons, markers, or glue and glitter.
(Be sure to talk about the meaning of the word pledge.)

11. Letter writing:
Have the students pretend to be Margo. Have them write a letter to Mrs. Baker apologizing for her behavior in class. *(Activity sheet 5.3)*

12. Caught You Being Honest Poster:
Prepare and laminate a poster with the title "I Caught You Being Honest." When a student observes another student in the classroom doing something honest, he/she will be allowed to write that person's name on the chart. He/she should also write the action of the person. Help them realize that this is a time of being honest themselves — not a time for best friends to pick best friends. This activity should encourage the students to be more aware of the actions of others and to practice honesty themselves.

13. Honesty Cards:
(Activity sheet 5.4) Divide the class into pairs. Give each pair of students a set of honesty cards. Have them read the situations and discuss with their partners what the characters should do to show honesty.

14. "Honesty Pays" (Sung to the tune of *Old MacDonald*)
Honesty, it really pays,
Really pays,
Really pays,
Honesty, it really pays,
It helps you get respect.

ACTIVITY SHEET 5.1

The Best Story Ever

©2003 YouthLight, Inc.

Character Analysis

PERSON	HONEST?	REASON	CONSEQUENCES

ACTIVITY SHEET 5.2

The Best Story Ever

©2003 YouthLight, Inc.

Directions: Write about a time that you were really proud of yourself for being honest. Be sure to include the **who, what, when, where, and why.** Give details. Use descriptive words.

_____

_____

_____

_____

_____

_____

_____

_____

_____

_____

_____

_____

ACTIVITY SHEET 5.3

The Best Story Ever

©2003 YouthLight, Inc.

Directions: Pretend you are Margo. Write a letter to Mrs. Baker apologizing for your behavior in class. You might try to explain why you behaved as you did.

ACTIVITY SHEET 5.4

The Best Story Ever

©2003 YouthLight, Inc.

Honesty Cards:

Grandmother and Grandfather live in another city. They like to reward you when you get good grades in class. They promised to give you $5.00 for each A that you earn. You usually get all A's. That means they will send you $30.00. This time you did not do so well. You only got two A's. Sam says, "You really were counting on the money to buy our camping equipment. Tell them you got all A's. They live so far away they'll never know." What should Sam do?

Seth and Laron are riding bikes down the street. They see a brown paper bag by the road. They stop and open it. They find it is filled with money. They take the money home and count it. There is $269.82. Seth's mother really needs money to buy groceries. What do you think the boys should do?

Cindy wants to go to the movies with Gloria. She has spent most of her allowance and does not have enough money. She asked her mother for some money but her mother said, "I'm sorry, Cindy. You chose to spend your allowance. You cannot go to the movies if you do not have the money."
Cindy know her little brother, Jake has money on his desk. He can't even count money yet and won't miss it if she took some. What should she do?

Bobby and Marcus sit by you in class. Mrs. Marks has an emergency and must leave the room for a short time. She says, "Class, I want everyone to finish the work that you are doing. If you are done before I return, please read in your library book. As soon as Mrs. Marks leaves the room, Bobby and Marcus begin to talk and work together. They finish first. Mrs. Marks returns to the room. Together you check the papers. Bobby and Marcus are the only ones to make 100. What should you do? What should they do? What should Mrs. Marks do?

STORY 6

Everyone Is Special

©2003 YouthLight, Inc.

SUMMARY:

Mrs. Vasquez assigned group projects for the class. This time she allowed the students to pick numbers for the group assignments. Martin always loved to work on projects but he loved to work with his best friend Danny. This time Danny is not in his group and Martin refuses to cooperate with his group. Mrs. Vasquez overhears Martin make an ugly remark about his group. She calls for a class meeting. During the class meeting, the students discuss the uniqueness of individuals and the importance of respecting all people.

ACTIVITIES:

1. **Self Portraits:**
   Give each child a piece of drawing paper. Have him/her draw and color a picture of himself/herself. Have him/her include in his/her picture as many identifying characteristics as possible such as freckles, moles, glasses, etc. Display the pictures in the classroom.

2. **Class Quilt:**
   Give each student a sheet of drawing paper. Have him/her draw and color a picture of himself/herself. When all the students are finished, group the pictures on a large piece of bulletin board paper and display it in the room. After displaying the quilt in the classroom, help the students identify individual differences of the students in the classroom.

3. **Book Sharing:**
   Share the book, Everyone Is Special with the students. After the book is finished, ask the class the following oral questions:
   A. Was Martin being a good citizen? Why or why not?
   B. Why did Mrs. Vasquez call for a class meeting? How was she feeling?
   C. Why do you think Mrs. Vasquez wanted to use a new way to divide the class into groups?
   D. Was this a fair way to divide into groups? Why or why not?
   E. What does it mean to be mentally challenged?
   F. What does it mean to be physically challenged?
   G. What did Mary Ruth find out about her new neighbor?

H. How do you think the students in Martin's group felt when he said, "They are dumb."
I. Did Martin learn anything in this story?
J. What does it mean to respect a person? Is this important? Why?
K. How do you feel if someone does not respect you?

These questions can be done orally with younger students or as a written activity with older students. (Activity Sheet 6.1)

4. **Everyone Is Special Song:** (Sung to the tune of *Twinkle, Twinkle, Little Star*)
I am special, you can see,
No one else is just like me.
I have two eyes, a mouth, and nose,
And a mind that grows and grows.
I am special, you can see.
No one else is just like me.

5. **I Am Special Necklaces:**
Cut small heart shapes from construction paper. Give each child five. Tell the students to write one thing that is special about themselves on each heart. When they are finished, have them decorate around the edge of each heart. Punch holes in the top of each heart. Give each child a piece of yarn about 15 inches long. Have the students string their hearts onto the yarn. Allow them to wear the necklaces to lunch.

6. **Individual Differences:**
During group time, have the students look around at each other. Have them look for ways they are all alike. Then, have them look for differences. This could be done using Venn Diagrams. Some venn diagram titles could be: Students With White Shoes and Students With Black Shoes, Students With Blond Hair and Freckles and Students With Brown Hair and Freckles, Etc.

7. **What's In a Name?**
Have each student write the letters of his name in acrostic format and write an acrostic for his name. *Example:*
Many different interests
Always on the go
Running from one thing to another
Tough to stop
In a flash
Never giving up.

STORY 6

Everyone Is Special

©2003 YouthLight, Inc.

8. Are You Special? (Sung to the tune of *Are You Sleeping?*)
Are you special? Are you special?
Let's just see. Let's just see.
Is anyone quite like you? Is anyone quite like you?
No, Sirree! No Sirree!

9. Kindness:
Point out that to emphasize that everyone is special, we must show kindness. This includes helping others and making them feel better. This not only makes the other person feel better but makes us feel better, too. This is sometimes called compassion. Have the students brainstorm ways they can show kindness or compassion. Make a poster of their suggestions.

10. Everyone Is Special Cards:
Divide the students into pairs. Give each pair several index cards. Have the pairs work together to draw or describe a situation that might need a kind or compassionate response such as: visiting a nursing home, a new student, a family who lost their home to a fire. When the cards are complete, have the students share the cards they made.

11. Adopt a Grandparent:
Plan a class field trip to a nursing home. Before the visit, have the class to make little favors for the residents. If the nursing home will allow, arrange for each child to "adopt a grandparent" at the facility. Then, throughout the school year, each student can write letters or make crafts for his adoptive grandparent.

12. Story Starters:
Use the following story starters as writing prompts in class or in the writing center of your classroom:

Once I was helped by _____
When a new person comes to class _____
When someone is unkind to me, I _____
I help others feel special by _____
Others help me feel special by _____

ACTIVITY SHEET 6.1

Everyone Is Special

©2003 YouthLight, Inc.

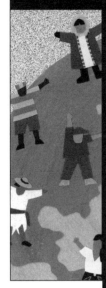

Directions:
Read the following questions about the story and write your answers in complete sentences.

1. Was Martin being a good citizen? Why or why not?

2. What does it mean to be mentally challenged?

3. What does it mean to be physically challenged?

4. What did Mary find out about her new neighbor?

5. Why do you think Mrs. Vasquez wanted to use a new way to divide the class into groups?

6. Was this a fair way to divide the class into groups? Why or why not?

7. Why did Mrs. Vasquez call for a class meeting? How was she feeling?

8. How do you think the students in Martin's group felt when he said, "They are dumb."

9. What does it mean to respect a person? Is this important? Why?

10. Did Martin learn anything in this story? If, yes, what did he learn?

ACTIVITY SHEET 6.2

Everyone Is Special

©2003 YouthLight, Inc.

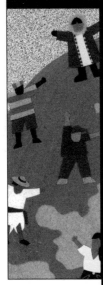

Directions: All the scrambled words below have to do with respecting the specialness of all people. Unscramble the scrambled words. Then write sentences with the words.

1. nssdknie _____

2. ptceesr _____

3. ndsiref _____

4. ringca _____

5. einc _____

6. nisglfee _____

7. reoths _____

8. lhlfeup _____

Note to the teacher: Cover the answers below before reproducing. For very young students, you may want to supply a word list for them to use as a reference. 1. kindness; 2. respect; 3. friends; 4. caring; 5. nice; 6. feelings; 7. others; 8. helpful;

STORY 7

D.C.'s Adventure

©2003 YouthLight, Inc.

SUMMARY:

D.C is a very irresponsible child. He leaves his towel on the bathroom floor. He leaves his toys wherever he finishes with them. He never puts away his toys. His mother continues to remind him of his responsibilities. School is no different. His desk is always a mess. He can never find his papers. His teacher, Mr. Cox, also reminds him of his responsibilities. D.C., after a particularly neglectful day falls asleep and has a frightening dream that convinces him that he is not being responsibible. From his dream he learns the importance of everyone accepting responsibility.

ACTIVITIES:

1. **Define Responsible:**
   Ask the children if they know the meaning of the word responsible. Write their responses on the chalkboard or on a chart. After they have made their responses, display these sentence strips in a prominent place:

   A. Being responsible is doing your best always.
   B. Being responsible is taking credit for your own mistakes instead of blaming others.
   C. Being responsible is being dependable.
   D. Being responsible for a job means that you get it done on time and correctly.

2. **Share the book *D.C.'s Adventures*:**
   After reading the book ask the students for ways that D. C. did not show responsibility. Ask them for ways that he did show responsibility. Ask them what made D.C. change his ways.

3. **I Am Responsible:**
   As a group have the students brainstorm things they are responsible for at school. Then have them brainstorm things they are responsible for at home. Ask them if it is important for them to complete their responsibilities and why.

D.C.'s Adventure

4. Class responsibilities:
With the students decide on a group project for which you, as a class, might be responsible. These might be:
A. Reading to students in a lower grade
B. Picking up litter on the school grounds
C. Tutoring younger students
D. Planting a school flower garden and caring for it
E. Becoming pen pals with nursing home residents

After the responsibility project is complete, have each student write a story about his/her experiences. Display the student work.

5. School Responsibilities:
Have the students brainstorm the responsibilities of the various workers in the school. These could include the principal, teachers, the counselor, teacher assistants, janitorial staff, secretaries, the nurse, media specialists, cafeteria workers, students, etc. Ask the students what effect there would be if these workers failed to perform their duties. Write the names of the individuals on little pieces of paper. Be sure you have one for each child even if you must duplicate the names. Place the names in a container. Have each child take a strip out. Instruct him/her to draw a picture of the school worker and write a story about that individual's work. Make a hall display of the artwork and stories.

6. Responsibility Flowers:
Prepare flower petals from construction paper. Give each child a paper plate. On the paper plate, have him/her write the words I am responsible. Give each child five or six of the prepared flower petals. On each of the flower petals, have him/her write one thing for which he/she is responsible. Attach the construction paper petals to the paper plates. Have him/her attach a stem and leaves to the flower. Display the flowers.

7. Field Trip:
Plan a field trip to the public library. Ask the media specialist to discuss how the library system is set up. Have this person explain the responsibilities of persons to take care of the borrowed materials and return them on time so others may borrow them also.

8. Responsibility Writing:
Write a letter to the students asking for someone who can be responsible to do a specific job. Have them write letters to you to convince you to pick them for the job. *(Activity Sheet 7.2)*

9. Person To Person:

To emphasize the importance of listening carefully and taking responsibility for your own actions, play this game. Each player selects a partner with one person remaining free to be the caller. The caller names two parts of the body which the partners must then try to have touch each other. For example, "nose to knee" would have the two partners bent over with their noses touching each other's knees. If the caller calls "person to person" everyone must change partners and the caller selects a partner also. The person left without a partner is the new caller. Some callers are inclined to stay the partner too long so a time limit may need to be imposed.

10. Composing:

Divide the class into groups of threes. Sing with them the song Twinkle, Twinkle, Little Star to make sure everyone remembers the lyrics and the melody. (Another song that they are familiar with would work also.) Ask the groups to compose songs about responsibility that can be sung to this tune. Allow them to share their songs when they are finished.

11. Responsibility Pledge:

Have the students complete the responsibility pledge *(Activity Sheet 7.3)* Encourage them to select an activity to do at home to show their responsibility for one week. Ask their parents to sign when they complete the responsibility each day. Collect at the end of the week and reward for good, responsible citizens.

12. Poetry Writing:

Divide the class into groups of two. Ask the students to write a poem with the title "We Get the Job Done. This poem should be about acting responsibly and working together. Allow them to share the completed poems.

ACTIVITY SHEET 7.1

D.C.'s Adventure

©2003 YouthLight, Inc.

Directions: Put the sentences in the correct sequence according to the story.

_____ D.C. was fast asleep and dreaming.

_____ D.C. heard the captain say, "If only you had cleaned your desk."

_____ At school the first thing D.C. did was clean out his desk.

_____ Just as the steamship neared home, he heard, "D.C., get up."

_____ He dropped the wet towel on the wet floor with his dirty clothes.

• •

Directions: Circle the right answer.

1. A responsible person   picks up his/her own toys.
                                           waits for someone else to pick up toys.

2. A responsible person   tries to remember what his/her homework is.
                                           writes down all assignments.

3. A responsible person   blames others for his/her mistakes.
                                           never blames others for his/her mistakes.

4. A responsible person   is always in charge of everything.
                                           works well with friends.

5. A responsible person   gets the job done on time and correctly.
                                           says he/she forgot what to do.

6. A responsible person   is someone you can count on.
                                           always finishes first.

7. A responsible person   is always right.
                                           does his/her best work.

D.C.'s Adventure

ACTIVITY SHEET 7.2

D.C.'s Adventure

©2003 YouthLight, Inc.

Directions: Read my letter. Write me a letter in return explaining why you would be the best person for this job.

Dear Student,

    I am looking for a student who can be responsible for returning library books to the media center on Friday mornings. Please write a letter telling me why you are the right person for the job, and how you will show responsibility with this task.

_____,

_____

_____

_____

_____

_____

_____

_____

                                                 _____

                                                 _____

D.C.'s Adventure

ACTIVITY SHEET 7.3

D.C.'s Adventure

©2003 YouthLight, Inc.

Responsibility Pledge

Date _____

Dear Parents,

    Our class has been studying citizenship. We are learning about responsibility. Your child has pledged that he or she will be responsible for a task at home for the period of one week. Each day that your child shows responsibility with his/her task, please sign your name.

Please return this sheet by _____. Thanks.

Sincerely,

_____

Child's name _____

Responsibility _____

Student Signature _____

• •

Monday _____

Tuesday _____

Wednesday _____

Thursday _____

Friday _____

Saturday _____

Sunday _____

STORY 8

That's Mine! Keep Your Hands Off!

©2003 YouthLight, Inc.

SUMMARY:

Kesha is rude to her friends in the neighborhood when they ask her to play. She is rude to her younger sister when she asks to look at her book. When she is talking to her mother, she reveals that she is upset because she thinks no one in her class likes her. By her mother's clever questioning and guidance, Kesha discovers that the problem is her own. She has become a very bossy child who has been unwilling to share and take turns.

ACTIVITIES:

1. **Share the book *That's Mine! Keep Your Hands Off!*:**
   Have the students decribe the character Kesha. Ask if she showed good manners in her behavior. Have them give examples of when she used good manners and when she did not. Ask if they would like to have Kesha for a friend? If yes, or no, have them give reasons.

2. **Taking Turns:**
   A. Discuss with the students times away from school when we are asked to take turns. Write these on the board or a chart. Have them include times when we are waiting in line to buy tickets at a ballgame or movies, waiting our turn to bat, or to check out at a store.
   B. Have them think about the reaction of others if we broke into the line and pushed to the front.
   C. Ask if there is a law that says we can't break into the line. Then, re-stress the idea that this is usually just a rule of good manners and respecting the rights of other people.
   D. Have the students think of times at school that they are asked to take turns. List all of these. Discuss the consequences if we did not take turns. (Not just the discipline but the chaos it would create.)

STORY 8

That's Mine! Keep Your Hands Off!

3. Sing a Song: *"For a Better World"*
(Sung to the tune of *London Bridge*)

For a better world,
We wait our turn,
Wait our turn,
Wait our turn,
For a better world,
We wait our turn,
And respect other people.

4. Sharing:
Point out that in the book Kesha did not want to share her things. Lead the students to discover Kesha's reasons for not wishing to share her book, her swing, her bike, her markers, and her ideas. Then, ask if it was okay for Kesha not to want to share these items with others. Help them conclude that her attitude was the problem.

5. Role Play:
As a group have the students brainstorm things that should not be shared such as new items, valuables, special memory items, toothbrushes, hairbrushes, etc. Write these things on note cards. Divide the class into teams and allow them to role play kind ways to refuse to share these items with others.

6. You Decide:
Ask the students to read questions and decide if an item should be shared. If it should not, have them write a kind refusal. Younger students could do this orally. *(Worksheet 8.1)*

7. What Should I do?
Discuss with the students the importance of taking care of borrowed items. Give examples of damaged borrowed items and allow the students to decide what should be done. *(Activity Sheet 8.2)*

8. Think Before You Act:

Ask the students what it means to think before you act. Point out that often people make bad choices because they do not think before they do something and have not thought about the consequences of that behavior. Point out to the students that in the book, Kesha did not think before she acted. Her words and actions to her friends and her little sister were unkind and hurt their feelings. Tell the students to ask themselves questions like these: "Is it kind? Is it healthy? Is it safe? Is it the right thing to do?" These questions may be displayed in the classroom as a reminder. Allow the children to practice this activity with sample questions.
(Activity Sheet 8.3)

9. Now The News:

A. In this game the students pretend they are on-the spot reporters adding to a news story as it unfolds.

B. The students are seated in a circle.

C. The object of the game is for each player to add three words to a single story as it is passed around the group. The three words should help describe an incredible news story about someone who shares an item, refuses to share an item, takes turns, or refuses to take turns.

D. Begin the story slowly. For example, the first player might say "On Saturday afternoon"; the second player might add, "Anna bought a"; while the third player adds, "new video game." If someone gets stuck and can't think of something, come back later. Keep the game moving from player to player.

10. Writing:

Have the students choose partners. Allow them to choose a topic and write a story. Topics might be: "The day no one shared; It's my turn now!; Sally screams, "It's mine!"

11. *Are You Sharing?* (Sung to the tune of *"Are You Sleeping?"*)

Are you sharing?
Are you sharing?
As you should
As you should?
Share your things with others.
Share your things with others.
You'll feel good.
You'll feel good.

ACTIVITY SHEET 8.1

That's Mine! Keep Your Hands Off!

©2003 YouthLight, Inc.

Directions: Read each situation. Decide if you think the person should share. Write a sentence explaining the reason for your answer.

1. Barbara's grandmother gave Barbara the necklace she wore when she and Barbara's grandfather were married. Kaye called and asked if she could borrow the necklace to wear to a party. She said it would be perfect with her new red dress. Should Barbara allow her to borrow the necklace? Why or why not? _____
_____

2. Myra loves to watch old movies about dogs. Fred has the movie, "Old Yeller". Myra asks if she might take it home to watch it. Should Fred loan her the movie? Why or why not? _____
_____

3. Ike and Larry are working on a project in class. Ike cannot find his pencil. Larry has three pencils. Should he allow Ike to borrow one? Why or why not? _____
_____

4. Lisa is spending the night with Beth. At bedtime Lisa says, "Beth, I forgot my toothbrush. May I use yours? Should Beth allow her to borrow the toothbrush? Why or why not? _____
_____

5. Mandy and Lashanda play together all the time. One day Lashanda was admiring a doll that belonged to Linda, Mandy's sister. She said," "Oh, Mandy, may I please take it home to play with tonight. I promise to take very good care of it. Should Mandy allow her to borrow the doll? Why or why not? _____
_____

6. Ty and Marcus play on the same baseball team. Ty always brings his own bat to use. He calls it his "lucky bat". Marcus is not a very good hitter. One day he asks Ty to use his "lucky bat". Do you think Ty should allow him to use it? Why or why not? _____
_____

ACTIVITY SHEET 8.2

That's Mine! Keep Your Hands Off!

Directions: Read each story. Write a few sentences telling the person in the story what he/she should do.

1. Martinez lives next door to his best friend Hank. They share toys very often. One day Martinez borrowed Hank's newest GI Joe. When he was ready to return it the next day, he could not find the shoes for the GI Joe. What should Martinez do?

_____
_____
_____

2. It is the hottest day of the year. The class has been on the playground for twenty minutes. Everyone is very hot and very thirsty. When they come inside, Marie lines up with the rest of the students. Marlene, who is last in line says, "Marie, may I get in front of you? Marie really likes Marlene. What should she do?

_____
_____
_____

3. Cliff has three brothers and three sisters. His family has very little money to buy toys. His youngest little brother likes to take all the wheels off toy cars for some reason. Cliff loves to play at Sidney's house because Sidney is an only child and he has lots of toys. One day when Cliff's mom called him home, Sidney said, "Hey, Cliff, you can take my remote control jeep home with you tonight if you want." What should Cliff do?

_____
_____
_____

4. Karisha was playing in her room. She picked up her newest magic wand. She saw that it was broken. She knew that Denise, her friend, had played with it yesterday and that it was not broken before then. What should she do?

_____
_____
_____

©2003 YouthLight, Inc.

ACTIVITY SHEET 8.3

That's Mine! Keep Your Hands Off!

©2003 YouthLight, Inc.

Directions: Read each situation. Decide if the person is making a good choice. Remember the questions, "Is it kind? Is it safe? Is it healthy? Is it the right thing to do?"

1. The class has been divided into groups to brainstorm ways they show good citizenship. Lance, Lane, and Cynthia are in a group. Lance and Lane wanted to work with Tim. Instead of working with Cynthia, they both ignore her and make the list together. Are they making a good choice? How do you know?

_____

_____

_____

2. Ming is home by himself in the afternoons until his father gets home from work. When he first gets home, he must call his father. Then he is allowed to get a snack, do his homework, and watch TV. On the table in the kitchen is a bag of chocolate kisses with almonds. This is Ming's absolute favorite candy. He does not know to whom they belong. What should he do? How do you know?

_____

_____

_____

3. Trace and Bailey are playing soccer in the front yard. Trace kicks the ball and it rolls into the street. He runs after it as it continues to roll across the street. What do you think? What should he have done?

_____

_____

_____

4. Sharee forgot to study for her math test on Friday. When Mrs. Black gives out the math papers and the class begins to work, Sharee notices that Ann's paper is uncovered. She can see the answers and Ann always gets the best grades. What do you think Sharee should do? Why do you feel this way?

_____

_____

_____

STORY 9

Can I Help Save The World?

©2003 YouthLight, Inc.

SUMMARY:

Sara helped pick up garbage on the streets around her school. Sara is very upset by the carelessness of the people who litter. She shares this disappointment with her parents. They suggest a classroom project to help clean up the town. The idea grows and soon several classrooms of students and parent volunteers have Saturday workdays to clean up the town. People in the community become interested in the project and join them. Jane and her class learn the importance of taking care of the environment and, as a result, get their picture of their class on a billboard displayed at the city limits.

ACTIVITIES:

1. **Define Ecology:**
   Write the word ecology on the board. Have the students define the word. Allow the use of the dictionary to check their understanding of the word. *(According to Webster, it is the branch of biology that deals with the relations between living organisms and their environment)* Put the meaning on a chart or sentence strips. Have the students brainstorm reasons that we need to know about ecology. Write the suggestions on the chart.

2. **Share the book, *Can I Help Save the World?***
   A. Discuss the importance of the Sara's class' project.
   B. Ask the meaning of the balance of nature.
   C. Ask how the students, parents, and teachers showed good citizenship.

3. **Research Foods:**
   Assign a research project in which the students discover the various foods we eat that are roots, stems, leaves, seeds, and fruits. Have them choose and draw one of the foods growing in the ground with the part that is eaten labeled. Have them research the origin of the food. Allow the students to share their reports.

4. **Define herbivore, carnivore, and omnivore:**
   Ask the students to define the words according to the book. Write the meanings on a chart. Then have them brainstorm familiar animals and decide to which group the animals belong.

53

STORY 9

Can I Help Save The World?

©2003 YouthLight, Inc.

5. Book Making:
Have the students use the words herbivore, carnivore, and omnivore to make books. Encourage them to illustrate their books by drawing pictures of each kind of animal.

6. Food Chain:
Teach the basics of the food chain. If possible secure pictures from a science kit. Use pictures to show the result when one animal is removed from the food chain. Have the children conclude why it is important to protect all animals and plants.

7. Write thank you notes:
Have the students pretend to be those students in Mr. Echo's class. Give each a 9" by 12" piece of construction paper. Have them fold the paper in half to make a card. Have them decorate the outside. Then, have them write a thank you note to the parents who helped with the Saturday cleanup.

8. Sing a song: (Sung to the tune of *"He's Got the Whole World in His Hands"*)

Verse 1
He made the green plants on the earth,
He made the seaweed in the sea,
He made the trees that stand so tall,
To shade both you and me.

(chorus)
What a wonderful world he has made,
What a wonderful world he has made,
What a wonderful world he has made,
And gave to you and me.

Verse 2
He made the fish swimming in the sea,
He made the creatures in the grass,
He made big animals walking around,
And Birds flying through the air.

Chorus

Verse 3
He gave it all, yes, to us,
He gave it all, yes, to us.
He gave it all, Yes, to us,
And said, "Take care of it."

Chorus

9. Applauding Taking Care of the World:
Have prepared construction paper headbands and handprint patterns. Let each child cut out several handprints from the prepared patterns. Allow him/her to decorate the handprints as he/she desires showing our beautiful world. Have them tape or glue their handprints to their headbands. Allow them to wear the headbands in the classroom.

10. Community Guest:
Invite a person employed with the local agricultural department to come to class and share with the class the various farming that is done in your state. Have him/her explain how important it is to protect the environment and conserve our resources. Have students discuss the situations *(Activity Sheet 9.1)*.

11. Community clean up:
Help the students organize a community clean up day. Enlist parent and other school volunteers.

12. Pennant making:
Give each child a large triangular shaped piece of construction paper. Have each child write the words, "We Must Save Our World" on his/her paper. Then allow each child to decorate it as he/she sees fit. Use plastic straws or small, cut dowel sticks for the pennant sticks. Have him/her secure the banner to the stick or straw.

13. Adopt a park:
If a park is near the school, with the class adopt the park and keep trash out. Allow time for the students to enjoy the beauty of the park. (Be sure to provide plastic gloves and instruct the students to never pick up needles or glass.)

14. Save the World Pledge:
Have the children make and sign a pledge to be conservers of resources *(Activity Sheet 9.2)*.

ACTIVITY SHEET 9.1

Can I Help Save The World?

©2003 YouthLight, Inc.

Directions: Read the sentences. Answer yes if the person is showing good citizenship by helping take care of our world. Answer no if the person needs to work on their citizenship. Explain your answer.

1. John and his family are going on vacation. They place a paper bag in the car. They will put any garbage into it. Then, when they stop, they will put the garbage in the trash can. Are they good citizens?

_____
_____
_____

2. Jacob takes very good care of his teeth. He brushes them every morning and every night. While he is brushing his teeth, he allows the water to run until he is finished brushing. Is he showing good citizenship?

_____
_____
_____

3. The Jones family likes to watch TV. Their TV is on all day long, even when there is no one in the room where the TV is. Are they showing good citizenship?

_____
_____
_____

4. Sabrina and her family have a beautiful yard. Her father has planted many trees in the yard. Are they practicing good citizenship?

_____
_____
_____

5. Alex is very afraid of earthworms. One day he said to his mother, "I wish all earthworms were dead." Is he showing good citizenship?

_____
_____
_____

ACTIVITY SHEET 9.2

Can I Help Save The World?

©2003 YouthLight, Inc.

Save the World Pledge

I promise that I will be a good citizen by taking care of our natural resources. I will

_____
_____
_____
_____
_____
_____
_____
_____

Signed _____

Date _____

STORY 10

No Bath Tonight!

©2003 YouthLight, Inc.

SUMMARY:

Chase never wants a bath. He wants to eat lots of sugary foods and candy. He does not care to brush his teeth. One night his mom reminds him to get his bath. However, Chase did not get up from the sofa. Instead, he falls asleep and begins to dream. In his dream, he becomes a guest in the home of a little group of men. These little men eat nothing but candy and cookies. They do not bathe. They do not get exercise. The things Chase learns from his dream help him to change his habits and to understand the importance of personal hygiene.

ACTIVITIES:

1. **Brainstorming:**
   Have the students brainstorm the things we should do to take care of our bodies. Write the student responses on chart paper.

2. **Share the book:**
   A. Read the book, *No Bath Tonight* and discuss what happened to Chase.
   B. Recall the things Chase discovered that he should do to keep a healthy body. Add any things that he learned that have not already been named on the brainstorming chart that the students made.

3. **Define self-discipline:**
   Ask the students if they have ever heard the words self-discipline. If they have heard the words, ask them to tell the meaning. Allow time for responses. Show this already Prepared definition: Self discipline means making good choices and having control over your actions and thoughts. It also means practicing good health habits. Explain that they are going to be studying healthy habits that everyone needs to practice to make healthy bodies that last for a life time.

4. **Bodies Need To Last:**
   Point out that the life expectancy for males in the United States is 74.1 years and for females it is 79.5 years. Help students discover just how long this is by helping them calculate how many days these years equal. Stress the importance of making good healthy choices now to grow good strong bodies for adult years.

5. Good Nutrition:
Discuss the meaning of the word nutrition.
   A. Ask the students to write down all the foods they eat in one day as a homework assignment. This should include all three meals and any snacks they may have. *(Activity sheet 10.1)*
   B. Show the students a chart of the basic food groups and discuss the foods they should eat each day. Have them compare their homework assignment of foods they ate to the basic food group chart.
   C. As a group make menus for one day including the proper amount of food from each of the basic food groups. Show the correct portion size. (The food group chart and models of serving sizes can be borrowed from the nutritionist at the local health department or agricultural extension office.) Older students may work in pairs to make healthy menus for one day that include the proper servings from each food group. Display the menus.

6. Sing a song: *Healthy Food*
(Sung to the tune of *Twinkle, Twinkle, Little Star*)

Are you eating,
Are you eating,
Healthy food,
Healthy food,
To build a stronger body,
To build a stronger body,
That lasts your life through,
That lasts your whole life through?

7. Dental Health:
   A. Secure and show the students models of primary and secondary teeth. Explain the purpose of primary teeth and that they are lost to be replaced by permanent ones. Point out that permanent means 74.1 years for a man and about 79.5 years for a woman. Help them conclude the importance of taking care of their teeth.
   B. If possible arrange for a dental hygienist from the local health department to come to class to demonstrate the proper techniques for brushing and flossing teeth. (Some health departments will furnish toothbrushes, toothpaste, and floss for each child.)
   C. Ask the students to sign the dental health pledge and take it home with them. Ask them to have their parents sign it each time they brush their teeth. After two weeks, reward those who return their papers signed and who have practiced good dental habits. *(Activity sheet 10.2)*

STORY 10

No Bath Tonight!

©2003 YouthLight, Inc.

8. **Sing a song:** *Are You Brushing?*
   (Sung to the tune of *Are You Sleeping?*)
   Are you brushing,
   Are you brushing,
   Everyday, Everyday?
   And are you flossing,
   And are you flossing,
   To stop tooth decay,
   To stop tooth decay?

9. **Physical Activity:**
   A. Brainstorm with the students how exercise helps the body. Write their responses on a chart.
   B. Divide the students into groups and ask them to research how physical activity affects the muscles, the bones, the heart and circulatory system, the lungs, and the brain. Have them share their findings. Add their findings to the brainstorming list.
   C. Mile a day club: Measure a distance on the playground that equals a mile. Work with the students at playtime building up their endurance until each student can run a mile. (Be sure to make a chart and record the names of the students as they complete the mile.)
   D. Jump rope: Help the students learn to jump rope — boys and girls.
   E. Organized games: Plan organized games in which the students have to run, hop, skip, do forward and backward rolls, etc. to develop muscles and physical strength.

10. **Sing a song:** *This Little Body of Mine*
    (Sung to the tune of *This Little Light of Mine*)
    This little body of mine,
    I'm going to make it move,
    This little body of mine,
    I'm going to make it move,
    This little body of mine,
    I'm going to make it move,
    Every day I'll make my body move.

11. **Drug Awareness:**
    A. Invite a police officer to present a drug awareness program.
    B. Invite a counselor with Alcohol Anonymous to present a program.
    C. Have the students sign pledges to remain drug free. (Activity Sheet 10.3)

12. Change Bad Habits Into Good Habits:

Discuss how we all have different habits or ways of doing things. Talk about some of the habits we have discovered that we need to work on such as flossing, brushing our teeth, eating the right foods, or getting the right amount of exercise. Have each child think about one habit he/she has that he/she would like to change. You might allow the students share the habits they wish to change with the class and their reason for wanting to change it. Have them tell what habit they want to put in its place.

Give each child a piece of 2" by 4" newsprint. Have him/her write on the newsprint the bad habit that he/she wants to replace. Have the students bring their written bad habits and follow you outside. Dig a hole and have the students place their bad habits in the hole. Cover the hole. Tell the class it will take time for the newsprint to decay and become part of the earth again. It also will take time for them to change an old habit into a new, better one.

Place a large rock over the place where the bad habits were buried. Have the students sign the rock with a permanent marker. When you return to the classroom, have the students sign the Watch Me Change card. *(Worksheet 10.4)*

After several weeks allow time for the students to reflect on how well they are doing changing the old habits. As new habits are established, bring the painted rock inside and plant flowers in its place.

13. Acrostic Writing:

Have the students write and share an acrostic for the word healthy.

H ___
E ___
A ___
L ___
T ___
H ___
Y ___

14. Story writing:

Have the students write stories about themselves and what they want their lives to be like fifty years from now. Have them draw a picture of themselves fifty years from now. Allow them to share the pictures and stories. Then display them.

15. Role Play:

Reproduce the self discipline cards onto heavy paper and cut them apart. Place the cards in a container and mix them up. Divide the class into small groups or pairs and ask each group to choose a situation from the container. Allow the students time to read the situation and talk it over. Have the students act out the cards. After each group has performed, have the rest of the class give suggestions that could show more self discipline. *(Activity sheet 10.5)*

ACTIVITY SHEET 10.1

No Bath Tonight!

©2003 YouthLight, Inc.

Dear Parents,

We are beginning a study of ways to develop healthy bodies. We will be studying proper nutrition, exercise, good dental hygiene, and drug awareness. We want to make the students become more aware of the foods they eat on a daily basis. We want you to help your child write down the foods they eat for one day including any snacks they eat. This is, in no way, to be judgmental of family practices but, instead, to help the students become more aware of food choices they need to make to promote healthy bodies.

Teacher Signature _____

• •

Date _____

Breakfast	Lunch	Dinner	Snacks

ACTIVITY SHEET 10.2

No Bath Tonight!

©2003 YouthLight, Inc.

Directions: Carefully read the pledge. If you agree to practice it, please sign your name and put the date.

Our Dental Health Pledge

I, _____, understand that my permanent teeth are meant to last a lifetime. I understand that to keep them healthy, I must brush twice a day with a good flouride toothpaste. I understand that I also should floss to remove any pieces of food stuck between my teeth.

Therefore, I promise on this the _____ day of _____, in the year _____, to brush my teeth twice every day and to floss my teeth once every day.

ACTIVITY SHEET 10.3

No Bath Tonight!

©2003 YouthLight, Inc.

Directions: Carefully read the pledge. If you agree to do what it says, please sign it and put the date.

Drug Free Pledge

I, _____, understand that alcohol and drugs are bad for my body and mind.

Therefore, I promise on this the _____ day of _____, in the year _____, to keep myself drug free. If I am asked to use drugs, I will say, "No, thanks. I love myself too much."

ACTIVITY SHEET 10.4

No Bath Tonight!

©2003 YouthLight, Inc.

Directions: Think of an old habit that you wish to change. Write it down. Then think of a new habit with which you will replace the old habit.

Watch Me Change My Old Habit
Into
A New and Better One

_____
_____
_____
_____
_____
_____
_____
_____
_____
_____

ACTIVITY SHEET 10.5

No Bath Tonight!

©2003 YouthLight, Inc.

Situation Cards

Amy does not like to go outside.
Instead she watches a lot of TV while she snacks.

Craig loves candy of all sorts.
His favorite snack is a great big chocolate candy bar.

Kizzy is playing at the park.
An older child comes up and begins to talk to Kizzy.
She says, "Hey, do you want some of my candy?"

Cassie won't stop talking in class.

Cindi is trying to develop better muscles
but when she runs, she is so tired.

Willie doesn't do his homework and
makes up an excuse.

ACTIVITY SHEET 10.5

No Bath Tonight!

©2003 YouthLight, Inc.

Situation Cards

Misty eats her cupcake first.
Then she is not hungry for anything else.

Anthony arrives late at school because he stayed up too late.

Marcy did not eat her breakfast this morning.
Now she can hardly think because she is so hungry.

Amy runs to get in line at the classroom door.

Marcus pouts because he can't have his way.

Kim asks a friend for the answer to a test question.

CITIZENSHIP
Certificate of Completion

This is to certify that

_____

has successfully completed

the activities for *Good Citizenship Counts*

on the _____

day of _____, _____.
            (month)   (year)

Teacher _____